In Pursuit of
Obedience

**Deepening our love for
God through obedience**

Steve Prokopchak

DEDICATION

This book is dedicated to those "fathers" and "mothers" in the Lord who have challenged me in my 30 year walk with God. They have helped to teach me obedience. Thank you for taking a chance on me.

I would like to thank all of those who have helped in the editing process. The following persons helped to make this book become a reality by their gifts: Mary, my wonderful wife. You are so busy and yet you give your time to me—I am blessed. Thanks to Sarah Mohler, Jenn Cox and Karen Ruiz of *House to House Publications* and to proofreader, Carolyn Sprague. You all have a special gift. And, thanks to Carolyn Schlicher, who not only serves as a prophetic intercessor for me and my family, but who has a command on the English language that I may never have. I especially appreciated Carolyn's help with chapter eight.

In Pursuit of Obedience

© 2002 by House to House Publications
1924 West Main St., Ephrata, Pennsylvania, 17522, USA
Tele: 800-848-5892
www.dcfi.org/house2house

ISBN: 1-886973-64-4

CONTENTS

Getting the Most from this Book 4

Before Getting Started 5

Foreword 7

1. Do We Love God Enough to Obey Him? 9

2. God Has Not Lowered His Standards 15

3. Wrong Reasons to Obey God 21

4. So, We Say We Love God 27

5. Pursuing Obedience 35

6. The Good News About Holiness 43

7. Humility—The Way to Holiness 49

8. Right Reasons to Obey 57

9. More Reasons to Obey 65

10. The Obedience Cycle 73

Getting the Most
from this Book

In Pursuit of Obedience is designed for both the individual reader and the small group study.

For the Individual

1. Begin each chapter with prayer and ask the Lord to help you understand its message and how to apply it to your life.
2. At the end of the chapter, a "Personal Growth Assignment" will help you to personalize the message.
3. Meditate further with the "Meditation Scripture for Obedience."

For the Small Group Study

1. Everyone reads the assigned chapter prior to the session so they are familiar with the topic.
2. At the start of the session, the small group leader opens with an "Ice-breaker" to help encourage relaxing interaction.
3. After prayer, begin with the "Thought Provoking Questions" to stimulate dialogue and participation in the small group setting.
4. The "Concluding Activity" helps to wrap up the session and allows participants to share what they have learned personally.

Before Getting Started

Have you ever felt overwhelmed about the tremendous act of self-discipline it takes to do what is outlined in scripture? Did you ever think that making good, responsible choices is too much to ask of yourself and others at times?

There are occasions when daily life can be a challenge, but for those who have decided to believe Jesus was who He said He was, there is a marvelous advantage to coping with life. We have God's love as both a foundation and fuel to guide us through any circumstance. This is not the *love* that the world's musicians sing about or claim to have mastered. This is something far more powerful.

Paul, in Ephesians 3:16-19, writes in awe at the fully unfathomable concept of God's love for us. He prays this prayer:

> I pray that out of his glorious riches he may strengthen you with power through his Spirit in your inner being, so that Christ may dwell in your hearts through faith. And I pray that you, being rooted and established in love, may have power, together with all the saints, to grasp how wide and long and high and deep is the love of Christ, and to know this love that surpasses knowledge—that you may be filled to the measure of all the fullness of God.

Why is it necessary to mention God's love in a book about obedience? Because even though we may struggle to experience on earth the full perfection of God's love, as well as sharing His love perfectly, His love for us must be the foundation upon which we build our emotional, physical and spiritual health. Any of the concepts in this book, taken alone and without the constant pursuit of growing deeper into His love, will make conviction turn into condemnation and true guilt into another "rule" to keep. We should love first, and then watch obedience follow. Do this, and you will understand why Jesus says His yoke is easy and His burden light!

God really desires us to obey. His commands do not grieve us because His commands are from a spirit of love. Do we love God enough to desire to obey Him only? I pray that through this study you encounter both of these meanings: loving His commands and knowing His love.

In Their Own Words

The short stories, called "In Their Own Words," at the start of each chapter are true narratives collected by the author, detailing people's experiences with obedience and disobedience. May we be encouraged by their stories as we see how obedience is the heart's reply to love—"This is love, that we walk according to His commandments" (2 John 6).

—Steve Prokopchak
DOVE Christian Fellowship Int'l
1924 West Main Street
Ephrata, Pennsylvania 17522

FOREWORD

When we look back on the American church of the 1990s and early 2000s, historians will probably comment on the casual attitude Christians had in those days. The church was so flippant about her mandate. We were so easygoing. We had it good, and we knew it. We had a pick-and-choose kind of faith. We were along for the ride, but we had little clue as to where we were going.

Yet throughout this era, God has sent voices to remind us that we can't keep this casual attitude forever. We were reminded that one day accountability would be required. One day, it would be obvious that the spiritual draft-dodgers and the casual inquirers would have to pay up.

We're closer to that time than we've ever been. And that's why I am glad my friend Steve Prokopchak has written this important book on obedience—a topic that American Christians have artfully avoided. I hope you will embrace this message and allow it to make you more sensitive to the voice of the Lord.

Does it matter if we listen to His voice? Can we afford to dismiss those quiet, yet powerful impressions we receive from the Holy Spirit? Can we ignore His warnings or push away His instructions? I don't think so. Yet so many of us do it every day. We dismiss His voice because we're too busy to obey, or because our lives are so cluttered that we have no room for His instructions.

Steve Prokopchak outlines for you in this book the importance of obedience, and with great pastoral sensitivity he offers hope and forgiveness to all of us who have failed in our attempts to respond to the Lord properly. Steve does not force-feed this message on us with a legalistic edge. He woos us to embrace an intimacy with the Father.

This book makes me want to turn my ear toward the throneroom and listen more carefully. I hope it will have the same effect on you.

—J. Lee Grady, editor of *Charisma Magazine*

We Don't Know the Day

Nicky rode dirt bike and so did I. One weekend I found myself with little to do. A voice inside me clearly said, "Call Nicky and see if he wants to go riding." I hardly knew the kid. He was my mechanic's son. I may have talked to him several times, but why would he ride with me? I dismissed the thought as a bit ridiculous and went off riding by myself.

Monday morning I heard some disturbing news. Nicky was coming home late Sunday evening after a date with his girlfriend traveling too fast for the mountain road he was on. Nicky rolled his dad's truck several times and was thrown from the vehicle. He was pronounced dead on arrival at the hospital.

I believe I missed an opportunity God wanted to give me, and I have regretted it ever since. At Nicky's funeral, I told Jesus I was sorry....I told Nicky too.

Do We Love God Enough
To Obey Him?

Maggie is a fornicator. And yet, she has never been acquainted with sin. Some tell me she is not really responsible for her actions. After all, I am told, "it's only natural." It is a funny thing, though. She does not even claim to be a victim—a victim of her parents, her younger years, her friends, her boyfriend, her family, her environment, or any of the cards that have been dealt to her in this life. I have never heard her blame anyone for what happened. In fact, I have never heard her blame anyone for anything that has come her way in the last 56 years.

Boundaries are "love limits"

Maggie is our 8-year-old yellow labrador retriever (that's 56 people years)! While my friends have encouraged me that Maggie is just being a dog, I am not convinced. Since six weeks of age, she has resided with our family. She has been trained to not stray into the neighboring yards. No matter how many children are playing and having a riotous time down the street, she knows it is "off limits" for her. Maggie was given boundaries to follow. She chose not to follow those boundaries. The lure of playful attention was too much for her—she chose to cross the line.

While I do not believe her pregnancy was intentional, she apparently found herself at the wrong place at the wrong time. Doing what comes "natural" has its consequences as well.

"But God wants us to be happy, doesn't He?" some question. "I know the Word of God says that, but after all..." is another line I often hear. When we adopt this attitude, it is like saying, "Yes, Jesus, we love You, but we also love wandering off into our neighbor's property!" Even though our God—full of love, compassion, and understanding—wants us to enjoy life to its fullest, He has always had boundaries for His people.

Boundaries are *limits* and *limits* are *love* when derived from a spirit of love rather than a spirit of control. When I set a limit for one of my children, it is because I love him and have his best interests in mind. Does God set limits for us because He desires to control us or because He loves us? His love for us is not in question; our love for Him is what is in question. Do you love Him enough to obey Him or, when the limit is "uncomfortable" for you, do you desire to rewrite the already written Word of God? While we're only at the beginning of this book, this is the most crucial issue when dealing with obedience. Let's consider this question again. Is your heart's desire to obey Him even when it gets uncomfortable?

Excuses we make

I have been supported for full-time ministry since 1977 and have heard many different excuses for sin; I've even used a few of them myself. We make excuses for not tithing; we make excuses for our affairs with ministry, jobs, money, things and persons other than our spouse. We make excuses for not attending fellowship, and we make excuses for not spending time in God's Word and prayer. Excuses do not hold up with God. Adam and Eve made excuses after the fall (Genesis 3:10,12,13). Peter denied his Lord and excused his behavior by saying, "I don't know or understand what you're talking about..." (Mark 14:68).

The Pharisees in Jesus' day were great excuse-makers as well. Jesus would often confront them when they attempted to appear very pious and religious on the surface. It was not surface responses that Jesus was looking for. He had a way of looking straight into their hearts, their personal motivation. It is interesting how the Pharisees, the religious ones of Jesus' day, could attack Jesus' disciples for picking grains of wheat to eat on the Sabbath. They thought they were upholding the law by being a sort of "religious police."

In Pursuit of Obedience

Then, just a few verses later, they were plotting about how they might kill Jesus (Matthew 12:1-43).

Did you ever feel like a Pharisee? On the outside, you desire to demonstrate a heart to obey God, all the while inwardly you find yourself wondering what is excusable and what is not. I have felt like a hypocritical "Pharisee" at times. Like Paul, I too could say my spirit is willing but my flesh is weak (Romans 7:7-25). The worst scenario is when I see a fault in my brother in Christ (a splinter) and cannot see the log jam in my own life. To be honest, I think the enemy of our soul, Satan, accuses every believer of being a hypocrite. It is a tactic he often employs to get us to compare ourselves. Feeling like a "fake" as we walk out the Christian life can be pretty normal.

This feeling, however, does not negate the fact that we are responsible to be honest with our God, ourselves, and our spiritual leaders. If we find ourselves thinking, "What can I get away with?" versus "What does God desire in my life?" we can get very close to that pharisaical view of life.

Obedience required

The United States government gave me the opportunity to learn so much while serving in the U.S. Air Force during the Vietnam era from 1972 to 1976. One memory I have was waking up the first morning of boot camp in that gray, narrow, metal military bed. As new recruits, we traveled all the previous day to get to Texas and then were screamed at and berated for hours until 2:00 in the morning. We were then told, "Get a good night of sleep and don't mess up the perfect 45° angles on the beds!"

At exactly 5:00 AM, three very brief hours later, a trash can came flying down the aisle with a big, mean, loud and intimidating drill sergeant behind it. "Get up, ladies!" were the first words out of his mouth. I didn't know if some women entered the barracks in the last three hours, but I was not going to look around. I flew out of bed and was practically dressed before my feet hit the ground. No one knew how to stand at attention, but with groggy minds and blurry eyes, we were awkwardly making our best attempt. That is—all of us but Airman Lucas.

For the rest of my life I'll never forget what happened that first morning. I was convinced that I was about to witness my first murder. Airman Lucas did not get out of bed. In fact, upon hearing all of the commotion, he hunkered down and pulled the covers over his head. Apparently, wherever it was that he came from, it was not yet time to rise and shine.

Sgt. Matthews advanced to Airman Lucas' bed, leaned over to where his ear might be located under the covers and barked with neck veins bulging, "I told you, airman, to get your @%#$ (backside) out of bed or I'll throw you out!"

Airman Lucas stirred, but did not remove himself from that bed. Forty-nine new recruits attempted to pretend we were not looking, but we all wondered what would come next. We did not have long to wait. Within seconds, Airman Lucas' bed, with Airman Lucas in it, was flying against the wall lockers.

From that day on, every other recruit in that military barracks came to a profound realization: excuses will not be tolerated—do not even try it. There was no excuse for shoes not properly "spit" shined, a bed not made perfectly or not obeying an order. The training was given, the military code of conduct was studied, and one had better not cross the line. Excuses were treated like contraband—immediately discarded.

Even our Lord indicated that there are wise and foolish builders. The wise persons build on a strong foundation while foolish builders build right on top of the ground. When the floods come, excuses will not work; the house will collapse. Jesus said these are persons who hear His words but fail to put them into practice (see Luke 6:46-49). Excuse makers hear the words, but fail to make practical use of them.

Personal Growth Assignment

On a small sheet of paper, write a boundary that you know you have a hard time accepting. On another sheet of paper, write the words "It is for my ultimate protection." Tape the second paper over the first, covering the boundary you struggle with. Carry this paper with you in your wallet, coat pocket, purse, backpack, etc. Each time you see it, remind yourself that this boundary is His covering of protection for you.

Meditation Scripture for Obedience

1 John 3:24; 5:2,3

In Pursuit of Obedience

Icebreaker

Have each person in the room name in one sentence an animal they are most like and why.

Open with Prayer

Thought Provoking Questions

1. What is an established boundary in your life that you are tempted to cross at times?

   For what reason do you believe you are tempted to cross the boundary?

2. Read Genesis 3:10-13. What excuses did Adam and Eve make for their disobedience? Read Mark 14:68. How did Peter excuse his denial of the Lord? What is the best excuse you have ever heard someone make for his or her sin? What is one you have made?

3. Name a way in which the boundary you listed in question one provides physical or emotional protection to you.

4. Read Luke 6:46-49. What does Jesus say about those who hear His words but fail to put them into practice?

Concluding Activity

Break into groups of three. Each person in the group should share in only two sentences what excuse he/she no longer wants to use in his life. The person to the right of the person who shared can then pray for that person and his need.

Obedience Pays Off

It had been a long week with my colicky baby, and I was sleep deprived. Along with that, my husband and I were finding ourselves at odds at practically everything as we adjusted to life with a first baby. He was goading me to get out of bed for church, but try as I might, I just couldn't bear the thought of getting ready, driving 45 minutes and sitting through a long service while I took the energy to listen and learn and worship.

"I won't go. I'm not going. Do what you want, but I'm staying right here." The thought of me saying these things with folded arms and a pout on my face, stubbornly clinging to sleep as my salvation brings a smile to my face even now. (Little did I know how many times I would see little faces in the same form reflected back at me in my future!) My husband, exasperated, simply left the room.

Then I heard it. Not loud, not booming, but gentle and calm. The complete opposite of how I felt and believed at the moment. "I want you to go this morning," was all He said.

I had promised I would obey Him as I learned to listen to Him speak to me. There it was. A choice to be made. He wanted me to go, even if I was sure I thought I knew the best thing for me that morning.

I chose to go, and the Holy Spirit moved in such an awesome, holy way on our church that morning that I experienced the presence of the Lord more intimately than most times He has met me. It was a life changing morning. How glad I am that I listened and obeyed!

2

God Has Not Lowered
His Standards

God does not tolerate sin, so why do we often live as though He has lowered His standard of holiness? Maybe it is because the adulterer is no longer stoned for adultery or the teenager for rebellion. Do these times of tolerance and lack of moral guidance in our culture cause us to question God's standard, His limits for our lives? We should never take advantage of God's grace by lowering our standards.

In today's world, the scripture, "I am the Lord, I change not" is viewed more like, "I am an understanding, benevolent, vacillating God who may or may not be upset with you and your sin." What is wrong with this picture? Has God lowered His standards because His creation cannot maintain a standard of holiness? (This is akin to our school systems in North America lowering the academic standard in order to have more students pass to the next grade level.)

Why do I read in Christian periodicals of the never ending list of divorced or divorcing leaders in the body of Christ? Like Maggie, they know the boundary is there. Unfortunately, *knowing* and *choosing* to maintain a heart commitment are two different matters.

In the Old Testament, we see that the Israelites were prone to follow the customs of the idolatrous and sinful people around them rather than obey God's laws. In Leviticus 20, God says He will severely judge those who refuse to obey.

> The Lord said to Moses, "Say to the Israelites: 'Any Israelite or any alien living in Israel who gives any of his children to Molech must be put to death. The people of the community are to stone him (v. 1,2). If anyone curses his father or mother, he must be put to death. He has cursed his father or his mother, and his blood will be on his own

head. If a man commits adultery with another man's wife—with the wife of his neighbor—both the adulterer and the adulteress must be put to death'" (v. 9,10).

You may say this sounds harsh, but how many piles of rocks in the front yards of American homes would it take to have teenagers begin to get serious about obeying their parents and the authorities that God has placed in their lives? How many rock piles would it take before adultery begins to decrease?

What has happened to "holy fear?"

Let's consider the case of a man named Ananias and his spouse Sapphira. This couple, mentioned in the book of Acts, decided to sell some of their property and give the money to the apostles. In the process, perhaps they received more for the land than expected or a spirit of greed knocked on the door of their hearts.

In any case, they schemed together to hold back a portion of the sale. The deception came when Ananias and Sapphira communicated that their gift was one hundred percent of the land proceeds. Peter confronted this deception by replying, "Ananias, how is it that Satan has so filled your heart that you have lied to the Holy Spirit...you have not lied to men but to God" (Acts 5:3,4).

What was the result of lying to the Holy Spirit? Ananias dropped to the ground dead. Within three hours, Sapphira showed up, recited the same lie and was laid to rest in her own freshly-dug grave beside her husband.

What was the reaction of those who witnessed this scene? "Great fear seized the whole church and all who heard about these events" (Acts 5:11). Could you hear the rumblings throughout the church for the next few weeks? Do you think anyone dared to lie to the Holy Spirit? Do you think anyone made any attempt to deceive the apostles? They most likely did not, for a holy fear seized the whole church. What has happened to this "holy fear" today?

Obedience is holiness; holiness is choosing obedience

Someone once said that the practice of holiness involves the pursuit of holiness. *When I choose to obey God's way, I choose the holy way.* I shudder to think where the Israelites would have found themselves if it had not been for a man named Moses. He had to be the greatest leader of all time. He was honest with God about his shortcomings, but he chose to steadfastly obey God. I get frustrated at times when reading the Old Testament and watching God's chosen people obey God—only to disobey, then obey and disobey again.

Let's take a look at Exodus chapter 14, verses 10 to 20. These verses relate a familiar story. Israel experienced miraculous deliverance out of Egypt by God. They now stand with their leader sandwiched between the uncrossable water of the Red Sea and Pharaoh's looming army of warriors, chariots, and earth-pounding horses. They can feel the ground trembling long before they can see their enemy. Clouds of dust from dry, desert sand is visible.

What is Israel's response? Is it with words of confidence and faith-assurance in their Deliverer?

Exodus 14:12 shows their fear and terror as they cry out to Moses, "Didn't we say to you in Egypt, 'Leave us alone; let us serve the Egyptians?' It would have been better for us to serve the Egyptians than to die in the desert!"

Moses tells the people to "stand firm" because the Lord would fight for them. However, God tells Moses to tell the people to "move." They have to move forward in faith toward the sea in order for God to deliver them. In the end, they obey the voice of God through His servant-leader Moses. While it is not without murmur and complaint, they do obey. That obedience leads them through the Red Sea on a dry sea floor. It must have been a very holy moment.

Who requires holiness? God does. Where does holiness begin? It begins with you and me. Holiness is choosing to be separate from the world and its sin. Holiness is an attitude of the heart. Pursuing holiness is obeying God. "The Lord said to Moses, speak to the entire assembly of Israel and say to them: 'Be holy because I, the Lord your God, am holy'" (Leviticus 19:2). Why must we obey God and pursue holiness? It is because we serve a God who is holy. This scripture from Leviticus is so important that we find it in the New Testament also:

> Therefore, prepare your minds for action: be self-controlled; set your hope fully on the grace to be given you when Jesus Christ is revealed. As obedient children, do not conform to the evil desires you had when you lived in ignorance. But just as he who called you is holy, so be holy in all you do; for it is written: "Be holy, because I am holy" (1 Peter 1:13-16).

Personal Growth Assignment
Set a timer for five minutes. Begin telling God sins you are aware of that you know you "get away with" because they are socially acceptable. Tell Him if you are ready to get rid of them. If you aren't ready to make that choice, tell Him. When the timer goes off, read 1 Peter 1:13-16 aloud.

Meditation Scripture for Obedience
1 Peter 1:22

Icebreaker

Go around the room and have each person share in four words or less the sin they think is most destructive to society.

Prayer

Discussion Questions

1. Name three standards God has set in the Bible that apply to relationships with other people. Why is it important that these standards be maintained?

2. Read Acts 5:3,4. What was the sin committed and what was the punishment? What was the reaction of the people around Ananias and Sapphira (Acts 5:11)?
   Name your "pet peeve" in terms of sins you dislike being committed. State what, if any, punishment you are aware of is outlined in scripture for this sin. What do you wish could happen each time this sin is committed that you think would teach the "sinner" a lesson?

3. Read 1 Peter 1:13-16. Why is being holy (or "set apart") so important to our relationship with God?

4. Explain why God not lowering His standards is important to understanding His true love for us.

Concluding Activity

Break into groups of two (same sex only). Each person should, without any discussion beforehand, pray a blessing over their partner. Ask God to give this person a new revelation of His holiness and of His deep, abiding love for them. Ask the Holy Spirit to bring to mind ways they can be more holy.

Pride Keeps Me From Obeying

The pastor was naming and claiming different illnesses and claimed he had an "anointing" for healing. This whole "Holy Spirit" healing thing was new to me, and I just wasn't too sure that God worked that way. However, I sensed something in the room that I couldn't define. Somehow I knew this was a changing time for the people going up front. It was a good thing I was so together that I didn't need to be crying in front of all these people. What would the leadership think of me if they saw a small group leader get up there and say I had a weakness that was hindering me?

The pastor went to the microphone again. He spoke of a person still in the audience who suffered from allergies, that it was serious and getting worse every year. A funny feeling came into the pit of my stomach, because I fit that description perfectly. "Surely there must be another person in the audience who suffers from allergies," I thought, and sat back in relief that I wouldn't have to go up after all.

Five minutes later, he was at the microphone again. This time, he felt the Lord telling him specifically that it was a woman suffering from the worsening allergies. "Surely God wouldn't have me learn about this new stuff by making me do something I'd be uncomfortable with," I reasoned.

Still a third time, the pastor got up, somewhat confused. He said again he was sure there was a woman in the audience who has allergies and was telling herself that it wasn't her that was to come up. I stubbornly refused to move and even felt a bit annoyed, "Surely if God wants to heal me, He can do it right here in my seat," I thought.

I suddenly felt a sensation of "withdrawing," as if I had been covered with a cozy blanket and it was lifted off of me. As I felt this, I realized my error and source of my sin. I began to cry, and told God I was wrong and asked if He would please still heal me.

It has been ten years, and I have prayed for many people and seen instantaneous deliverance from illnesses and emotional wounds. Yet this thorn remains in my flesh. God, in His mercy, is healing me through the use of desensitization shots and prescription medicine. My better wisdom now testifies that I wouldn't have had to spend these ten years and many dollars suffering, had I just obeyed His kind call when He offered.

CHAPTER

3
Wrong Reasons to Obey God

Before we continue our discussion of holiness, let's look at reasons some of us have chosen to obey God. Can you recall when you were young and your motivation to obey the authority in your life was based upon fear, a rule, trying to earn something or to escape from an undesirable situation? I can. It never produced a lasting desire to obey. It reminds me of the little boy who was told to sit down. While he obeyed the command and complied outwardly, he said, "But, I'm still standing up on the inside!"

One goal of a healthy, mature Christian is to obey God readily on the outside while our hearts are resting in a trust of God's concern for our welfare on the inside. Our love for God, as well as knowing God's love for us, draws us to obedience. That is our motivational factor. However, there are some negative forces motivating us to obey God. Let's look at a few of those.

Unwholesome fear

I once complained to a friend of mine that my children seemed to take too much liberty when it came to telling me what they thought. I shared with him, "You know, I would have never spoken that freely to my father." Wisely, my friend asked me if I feared my father when I was growing up. "You bet—don't we all?" was my quick retort.

I'll never forget his reply to me. "Steve, you were raised with an inappropriate fear of your father. Your sons know your unconditional love for them." Because my heart for my children is one of love and approval, they have not experienced an inappropriate fear within our relationship. At the same time, my children do not have a license to be disrespectful.

Fear is a great motivator, for sure. But our God chooses to motivate out of love. *I do not walk in an unhealthy fear of my heavenly Father because I know His unconditional love.* Fear of punishment is an inappropriate reason for obeying your heavenly Father.

Perhaps you discovered within the scripture that there is a healthy fear of the Lord. What is the difference with this type of fear? It is an important discussion at this point.

Rather than being afraid of God, this fear is one of reverence; it's a fear that recognizes God's awesomeness and holiness. Psalm 111:10 describes it this way, "The fear of the Lord is the beginning of wisdom; all who follow his precepts have good understanding..." There is a security within this appropriate fear. "He who fears the Lord has a secure fortress, and for his children it will be a refuge" (Proverbs 14:26).

It is this holy, awesome, and reverent fear of the Lord that actually draws us away from the unholy and from disobedience. "...Through the fear of the Lord a man avoids evil" (Proverbs 16:6).

The difference between a healthy fear and an unhealthy fear is clear. A healthy fear recognizes God's love for us and is life giving. "The fear of the Lord leads to life; then one rests content, untouched by trouble" (Proverbs 19:23). An unhealthy fear is connected to punishment. While we may deserve God's wrath and punishment for our sin, He placed it upon our crucified Savior. (For the scriptural account of this, please see Romans 5:6-11.)

Legalistic rules and regulations

Maggie spends most of her time in a six-by-eight foot kennel in which is a large, insulated, wooden dog house. She's given plenty of water and food. Yet, it is a funny thing: outside of her kennel she desires to run, roam, sniff and do those things dogs do. It is when she is loose that we need to keep a close eye on her. Without warning, she can just quietly disappear. No amount of calling will coax her to return. She vanishes!

On the other hand, I've observed dogs on farms that are allowed to roam freely wherever they like. Where do you often find them? There they are, lying on the front porch of the farm house or alongside the farmer as he goes about his daily chores.

Josh McDowell has repeatedly told us that rules and regulations without relationship cause rebellion. If God is simply reduced to a bunch of rules and regulations, void of any personal intervention in our lives, then what we have is dead religion. Dead religion is nothing more than incorporating all of the do's and don'ts of the particular religious hierarchy.

We choose to obey God out of having a healthy relationship with God and not because He maintains a little black book called a "grade book"! In the midst of the regulations of the Old Testament, it was Samuel who told King Saul, "Obedience is better than sacrifice" (1 Samuel 15:22). *Sacrifice came out of regulation; obedience comes out of love.* Obedience is doing all God wants me to do, while sacrifice is doing what I want to do for God. Paul stated it so succinctly when he wrote about the law and obedience in Romans 2:13, "For it is not those who hear the law who are righteous in God's sight, but it is those who obey the law who will be declared righteous."

To earn favor from God

If you are a parent, have you ever noticed a son or daughter becoming extremely compliant or extra "nice" only to discover your smiling teen has a special reason—to borrow the car? Maybe an employee is going out of his way to be unusually pleasant or helpful to you, his boss. At the end of the day you begin to put two and two together. The employee wants to leave early on Friday to get a head start on the weekend. What's wrong with this picture? And, what happens when we say no? We can liberally receive the cold shoulder, distance, or perhaps anger. You know how it goes because you can remember a time or two when you found yourself desiring a special favor from someone.

We don't fool God. After all, He knows our hearts. He knows what we're really thinking. He is not a politician running for office. He doesn't care if you vote for Him or not. He *is* Grace. You do not need to somehow get into His "good grace." You may fool some people with whom you relate, but you'll never fake out God. Ananias and Sapphira could not con Him. What makes us think we can?

You cannot earn God's favor. Do you know why? You already have God's favor, if you are a believer. We cannot earn something that has already been given to us! "Accept one another, then, just as *Christ accepted you,* in order to bring praise to God" (Romans 15:7).

To escape an undesirable life situation

Why is it that the first two words out of the mouth of someone in a desperate situation is, "Oh, God!"? If you really did not care about obeying God when things were going well, why care now? Desperate persons see God as the proverbial "fire escape." They want to get as close to the fire as they can and then when it starts to burn, they need God.

The drug addict swears to God he will go straight: "Just get me out of this mess." The abuser tells the abused, "I am so sorry, please forgive me; it will never happen again. God, you've got to help me. I'll get counseling, anything, just don't tell anyone."

Contrition is not necessarily repentance. Contrition is a regret at being caught and says, "I'm caught—now I need your help, God." Repentance is a remorse for our action, desiring to change. It says, "Dear God, I'm not worthy to even look Your way. I am so vile, so lost, so disgustingly perverted in my heart and mind. I am truly sorry. Can You forgive me and set me on the course of obedience?"

God is not a fire escape so that we can glibly do an "about face" after He intervenes in our life and yet maintain the same heart attitude. *Jesus has already made our way of escape; obeying Him means to follow Him in that way.*

There was an unnamed woman in Luke eleven who blurted out some words about Jesus when He was teaching one day. She said of Him, "Blessed is the mother who gave you birth and nursed you" (verse 27).

Was this a reason to follow and obey the Savior? Jesus' response was interesting: "Blessed rather are those who hear the word of God and obey it" (verse 28).

Personal Growth Assignment

Reflect for two or three minutes on the discipline your parents used when you broke a house rule. Try to connect whether this has carried over to a wrong reason you have for obeying God. If it has, ask God for a fresh understanding of His parenting skills. If no, write your parents a quick thank you for their loving training to you.

Meditation Scripture for Obedience

Acts 5:29

Icebreaker

Have each person in the room tell the one traffic law they wish they didn't have to obey.

Prayer

Discussion Questions

1. Name the four wrong reasons for obeying God. Which is the one you use most? Why? Are there any other wrong reasons for obeying God? What are they?

2. Obeying because we have an unhealthy fear that is connected to punishment is a wrong reason to obey God. We may deserve God's punishment, but read Romans 5:6-11 to see how we escape this punishment.

3. Read Psalm 111:10; Proverbs 14:26; Proverbs 16:6 and discuss the elements of a reverent fear of God.

3. Name two ways you can prevent a wrong reason from motivating you to obey. Ask others in the group to suggest other ways to prevent wrong reasons from motivating you.

4. How can reflecting on God's love for you change your thought patterns when you realize you are obeying God for the wrong reason(s)?

Concluding Activity

Break into groups of four. Each person should share which "wrong reason for obeying God" he/she most identifies with. Immediately after sharing, pray for each other, speaking Philippians 4:13 over each person, "_____ [name of person] can do all things through Christ who strengthens him/her."

Disobedience "Nailed" Me

"I really should be cutting these apart on my miter saw," I thought to myself as I stomped on another piece of door trim to break it up for the garbage. "All these nails sticking out might hurt me." Again, I stomped on an eight-foot piece and very gently heard, "You should stop doing it this way." There were just a few pieces left, and I really wanted to get on with cleaning up the garage. I lifted my knee and took my work boot down on the next one. A nail pierced my flesh with excruciating pain!

As I gritted my teeth while my wife quietly poured peroxide into a container, I told her I had received a warning about this happening. I wasn't sure which stung more—the puncture that went clear to my heel bone, or knowing I could have avoided this pain had I only listened.

4

So, We Say We Love God...

What does it mean when we say we love God? When my child comes and says, "I love you, Daddy," and immediately proceeds to disobey me, is that "loving Daddy?" If I say I love God, what am I actually saying? Let me answer this question with several key and pointed scriptures:

This is love for God to obey his commands... (1 John 5:3).

And this is love that we walk in obedience to his commands...(2 John 6).

If you love me [Jesus said], you will obey what I command (John 14:15).

Whoever has my commands and obeys them, he is the one who loves me... (John 14:21).

Obedience is connected to love

What is connected to love? Obedience is. How do I know my children truly love me? It is by their obedience to me. How does God know we truly love Him? It is by our obedience to Him.

As a home cell group leader in our cell-based church, I can recall the time when I felt the Lord was asking me to allow our 12-year-old group to dissolve. While twelve years may be a long time, the cell group had successfully multiplied many times. However, it had now become a "grandparent," unable to reproduce. I felt that if the group would dissolve (die), God would resurrect something of life from it.

When I shared with my wife and assistant cell leaders this impression from God, no one agreed with me. Being outnumbered, I figured that perhaps I had "missed" God. Within a short time, a couple came forward and expressed a desire to start a new group.

"Perhaps I was wrong about dissolving the cell," I thought, "now the group will multiply with this couple as the new leaders."

Several months went by and still there was no multiplication. People began to leave the cell, and the couple that expressed a desire to start a new cell left and began attending another. What was happening? While making an appropriate effort to listen to others who had the right to speak into the situation and maintain accountability, I disobeyed God. It wasn't long until the others also saw the need to dissolve the cell.

In the end, perhaps the timing worked out for the best. But I had begun to see some immediate results of attrition within the cell. To this day, I connect that weakening of the group to not acting soon enough in obedience to God's prompting.

What happens when we are lethargic in our obedience

I realize there is a major difference between God's abundant grace and our lack of immediate obedience.[1] The difference might be that we become lethargic in our obedience. Even children can be observed taking their liberty well over the line when the line is not watched carefully or reinforced by the parent. *It is thinking we're getting away with something that can actually keep us motivated toward disobedience.* If we see no immediate reward or punishment for our behavior, lethargy can set in. We might ask ourselves, "Does anyone really care?" Ultimately, if we are more concerned about how we feel than what God states in His Word, it's easy to see that obedience to God is not our highest priority. Our own self desire takes highest priority.

Jeff, (not his real name) a personal friend of mine, asked to meet with me at my office as soon as possible. Jeff had been in a missionary type ministry for many years. As he shared his story, I had a hard time believing the person sitting across from me was the person that I thought I knew. Jeff cried when he shared how he found himself involved in some very non-Christian activities. He had disappointed his wife, his Lord, and himself. He had no answer to the "why" question, only regret.

Jeff's disobedience had so affected him that he now suffered from depression and numerous physical conditions. Although he was presently being treated by a doctor, he knew the origin of these physical ailments was in the soul—the emotional realm.

28

When I asked Jeff where it all began, he had a very clear response. "I had been hurting for some time," he said. "I tried to reveal this to several persons close to me numerous times. No one seemed to take me seriously; no one came forward to offer any help. I then began to dabble in sin and thought that revealing these things would surely get someone's attention. This time, they recommended a month off. They thought I must be 'burned out.' This time off was supposed to help me with my physical condition as well."

Jeff continued, "The month off was good, but noneffective. I wasn't dealing with my disappointment in ministry, my frustrations with staff, my sinful musings and attractions. My family and I took some time away, but I had no one working with me, confronting me and the inner struggle I was going through."

"My wife blamed it all on the ministry as she sided with me, but I wasn't convinced," Jeff revealed. "I knew I had a choice in my disobedience, but for the life of me wondered whether anyone really cared about me, or was their only concern the ministry?"

Finally, the truth about Jeff's ongoing sin came out when he stated, "The more I sinned, the easier it became, and the less accountable I was. It was like a game for me, and I continued to win at it." Now, sitting with me, he realized he was losing the game—physically, emotionally and spiritually.

Taking advantage of God's grace
Sometimes it seems we may take advantage of God's grace by our own fleshly, selfish desire. "I want what I want" are five of the most self-centered, self-destructive words of immaturity. James states it this way: "Such 'wisdom' does not come down from heaven but is earthly, unspiritual, of the devil. For where you have envy and *selfish ambition*, there you find disorder and every evil practice" (James 3:15,16).

While selfish ambition may be the "wisdom" of this world, it certainly is not of God's world. The fruit of our selfishness is "disorder" and "every evil practice." This does not sound too inviting. In James 4, there is a very clear and illuminating exemplification of selfish motives: "You want something but you don't get it. You kill and covet, but you cannot have what you want. You quarrel and fight. You do not have, because you do not ask God. When you ask, you do not receive, because you ask with wrong motives, that you may spend what you get on your pleasures" (James 4:2,3).

In these verses, the "wrong motives" are clearly connected to our own personal selfish desires. When we are self-seeking, we are not at the same time God-seeking. In Galatians 2:20, Paul wrote that we are to be "crucified with Christ," in other words, crucifying our selfish desires, he also wrote that we should not "frustrate the grace of God" (verse 21). How do we frustrate God's marvelous, life-giving grace? It is by leaning on our own self-righteousness.

When George Barna studied divorce by surveying 3,142 randomly selected adults, he found the divorce rate higher among those who claimed to be born-again Christians (27%) than among those who did not claim any faith in Christ (24%).[2] Having a heart for marriage and working fervently to see married persons stay married, I found myself extremely frustrated with these statistics.

What are we thinking? Has God changed His standard? Do we so take advantage of grace that we are okay with disobedience? God's grace does not nor will it ever absolve our need to obey Him. Author Larry Kreider, in his Biblical Foundation Series book entitled, *Living in the Grace of God*, writes:

> If God is so willing to forgive sin, and since Christians are under grace and not the law, does this mean we can continue to tolerate sin in our lives and yet remain secure from judgment? After all, God's grace pardons sin. We can sin because God will always forgive us, right? Wrong! This is the very issue the early church ran into. Paul challenges this train of thought that "cheapens" God's grace: *What shall we say, then? Shall we go on sinning so that grace may increase? By no means! We died to sin; how can we live in it any longer? (Romans 6:1)* It is a distortion of God's grace to think we can continue to live in sin and God's grace will cover it.[3]

If it did not work for Ananias and Sapphira, or Judas, or King David of old, what makes us think that it will work for us? *God, give us "the fear of the Lord" and a heart to obey You quickly!*

As twenty-first century Christians, we would be blessed to pray a prayer written by A.W. Tozer. Are you thirsty for quick obedience to your God?

O God, I have tasted Thy goodness, and it has both satisfied me and made me thirsty for more. I am painfully conscious of my need of further grace. I am ashamed of my lack of desire. O God, the Truine God, I want to want Thee; I long to be filled with longing; I thirst to be made more thirsty still. Show me Thy glory, I pray Thee, that so I may know Thee indeed. Begin in mercy a new work of love within me. Say to my soul, "Rise up, my love, my fair one, and come away." Then give me grace to rise and follow Thee up from this misty lowland where I have wandered so long. In Jesus' name. Amen.[4]

Personal Growth Assignment

Ask the Holy Spirit to point out to you a specific way you disobeyed God in the last seven days. Speak out the sentence, "I have disobeyed God by _____ ." Now, turn to John 14:21 and substitute your name for the "anyone" in the verse.

Meditation Scripture for Obedience

1 John 2:3-6

[1] For an excellent book on grace, see Philip Yancey's book entitled *What's So Amazing About Grace*, Zondervan, 1997.
[2] *Marriage Partnership Magazine,* Jim Killam, Summer 1997, pp. 46-48.
[3] *Living in the Grace of God*, Biblical Foundation Series, Larry Kreider, (Ephrata, PA: House to House Publications, 2002), p. 36.
[4] *Tozer on Christian Leadership,* Ron Eggert, (Camp Hill, PA: Christian Publications, Inc., 2001), p.11.

Icebreaker

Go around the room and have everyone give a one sentence definition of the word "grace."

Discussion Questions

1. Talk about one time you knew God was telling you to do/not do something and you disobeyed Him. How is knowing God is full of grace toward you helpful in remembering this time?

2. Now, talk about a time that you clearly did what He commanded. What was the result?

3. How does remembering these times encourage you to obey Him in the future?

4. How can we take advantage of God's grace and what can happen according to James 3:15,16?

5. What do we crucify when we are "crucified with Christ" (Galatians 2:20)?

Concluding Activity

Break into groups of three. Have each person describe how they would like to deepen their understanding of God's grace. Also, have each person share a victory in the area of disobedience in their own lives they've had in the past four weeks. Pray together as a group, but instead of asking God for anything, thank Him for at least three praiseworthy things that stand out to you about this session.

Pleasing God, Not Man

I had a choice: obey God and lose the respect and admiration of man or obey man and lose God's immediate call in my life.

It was 1977, and we had been married for two short years. With no children and two good jobs, my wife and I had no needs or wants. We were secure, living in our little corner of the world. And then it happened. We heard the voice of the Lord calling us to full-time youth work where we would not receive a pay check, but would live by faith. How exciting and scary it was.

The day came to inform my parents. "What? ..... to move where? ..... and give up your jobs? ..... to live by what? ..... none of this makes any sense..... I can't support you in this ludicrous decision," was my father's response. I was a young, immature married man now wondering if I heard God correctly. I had to search my heart while asking myself whose approval I was really looking for.

"They loaded up the truck and they moved to Beverly" as the TV show song goes. The next eight years, God confirmed His will by our obedience over and over again by His provision and care for us. With or without a paycheck, we were never found to be begging for bread. It's fulfilling to obey God with or without the admiration of men.

5

Pursuing Obedience

To what extent was Jesus obedient? The scripture states, "And being found in appearance as a man, he humbled himself and became *obedient to death*—even death on a cross!" (Philippians 2:8). Jesus was so obedient to the Father that He suffered, bled, and died in obedience.

How successful did Jesus look when He was hanging from the cross? Not very. However, it was not success that He was in pursuit of; it was obedience. From the cross, He cried out to the Father, "It is finished." He obeyed His Father to the end, which for us meant the beginning—in fact, it meant everything for us.

Never wavering

His obedience brought forth our salvation, our promise of life after death—resurrection life. I'm so grateful that Jesus did not become lethargic about obedience. He never wavered, regardless of Israel's lack of faith,[1] despite the attempts of the Pharisees to test Him,[2] when people sneered at Him,[3] knowing that a disciple would turn against Him,[4] and regardless of the pain, suffering, and humiliation that He would endure.[5]

A wonderful dialogue between Jesus and His Father takes place in John 17. I believe it will illustrate our Lord's heart to obey. In verse 4, Jesus states that He has completed the work that the Father gave Him to do on this earth and brought His Father glory in the process. Other expressions of obedience from that chapter follow:

[6] I have revealed You to those whom You gave me....

[7] For I gave them the words You gave me...

[8] All I have is Yours...

[9]...I protected them and kept them safe by that name You gave me.

[10] I have given them Your word...

[11] As You sent me into the world...

[12] I have given them the glory that You gave me, that they may be one as We are one.

[13] I have made You known to them, and will continue to make You known...

Not hypocritical

We have discovered by now that Jesus was not popular among the religious people of His day. They seemed to be in constant conflict with His healings, His stories, His life. Just what was the difference? Why was there so much division between the two?

In John 8:28, Jesus states to the Pharisees, "I do nothing on my own but speak just what the Father has taught me." Were the Pharisees following their own selfish, religious, prideful, need-to-be-seen-by-men desires and then speaking from that platform? I believe they were, and while they may have fooled many people of their day, the Son of God was so full of the Spirit of God that He saw right through their narcissistic religion. "You are from below; I am from above. You are of this world, I am not of this world." Jesus candidly revealed the nature of their own hearts to them (John 8:23).

Using another Pharisaical illustration, Matthew 15 records a time when Jesus called the Pharisees hypocrites. He then quoted the prophet Isaiah saying, "These people honor me with their lips, but their hearts are far from me" (Matthew 15:8).

We can look like we are obedient. We can speak words of obedience with our lips, but our Lord knows our heart. The Pharisees thought they were okay with God if they kept the religious traditions and the rules of man. Jesus, however, was not impressed and neither was He fooled.

Jesus' identity was so fully found in His Father that nothing and no one could deter Him from obedience. You see, we waver in our obedience when we feel that something may benefit us, our esteem, our approval before men or just to gratify our flesh. How do

In Pursuit of Obedience

I know our Lord's identity was so secure in His Father? John records more of Jesus' words when He spoke, "...for I know where I came from and where I am going" (John 8:14). This was His testimony. Every testimony needed to be established by two witnesses. Who was His witness? "My other witness is the Father who sent me" (John 8:18). But, wasn't this the same God (Father) of the Pharisees? "You do not know me or my Father, Jesus replied..." (John 8:19). While the Pharisees claimed to know God and even obey Him, it was the Spirit of truth and discernment that resided in Jesus which declared otherwise.

Distinguishing good from evil

The Pharisees with whom our Lord had confrontations were required by the Old Testament to maintain a very clear distinction between the holy and the common. The priests were instructed in Ezekiel 44:23 to "...teach my people the difference between the holy and the common and show them how to distinguish between the unclean and the clean." *Teach* and *show* were the commands. We need teaching (on holiness) and we need to be shown (mentored and discipled by spiritual parents) in order to be able to distinguish the unclean from the clean.

There is a New Testament principle that parallels with this thought. Hebrews 5:13, 14 shares, "Anyone who lives on milk, being still an infant, is not acquainted with the teaching about righteousness. But solid food is for the mature, who by constant use have trained themselves to distinguish good from evil." In our immaturity, we need milk. Could it possibly be that even though many of us are Christians for years, even decades, we still struggle with obedience because we are actually spiritual babies? *The mature are separated from the immature by their obedience.*

Older Christians who lack spiritual maturity are "adults in age" but "babies in spiritual growth." They may be 20, 30, 40 or 50 years of age, and have never spiritually matured. They live self-centered life-styles, complaining and fussing and throwing temper-tantrums when things do not go their way. Some do not accept the fact that God loves them for who they are. Others may wallow in self-pity when they fail. Still others may live under an immense cloud of guilt and condemnation.[14]

Holiness may seem so far from our reach because we've never really believed that we could be holy. However, as someone once said, to continue to walk in *unholiness* results in a lack of *wholeness*.

The book of Romans states this principle a little more candidly. In chapter six there is a reference to slavery and obedience. Let's look at verse 16, "Don't you know that when you offer yourselves to someone to obey him as slaves, you are slaves to the one whom you obey—whether you are slaves to sin, which leads to death, or to obedience, which leads to righteousness?" Obedience leads to righteousness, to holiness, and to maturity.

Pleasing God, not man

While the Pharisees knew the teaching of the holy and the common, their daily practice was to only conform to the law outwardly. Jesus told them, "You are the ones who justify yourselves in the eyes of man, but God knows your hearts..." (Luke 16:15a). Pride kept the Pharisees from taking an honest inward look. Self-justification was their drug of choice.

Pride is often at the center of our disobedience. How does a spirit of pride which is self-preservation keep us from pursuing obedience?

A spirit of pride causes us to think we are pursuing our own personal identity and worth by looking good before others, especially those we admire. The Pharisees continually attempted to save face before one another and those who they desired to impress. Paul the apostle's observation about this was that when we are trying to justify ourselves, we are being alienated from Christ (Galatians 5:4).

Paul was surprised by the fact that the Galatian church could so easily and quickly be persuaded to believe another gospel (mixing an observance of the law with faith—Galatians 3:1-5). He asked the Galatian church some questions that if we were to answer today for ourselves could reveal a spirit of pride. He asks, "Am I now trying to win the approval of men or of God? (What does my desire to obey connect to—God's approval or man's approval?) Or, am I trying to please men?" (Galatians 1:10) Later, in chapter two, Paul separates himself from those who seemed to "be important" but, fully convinced that, "...God does not judge by external appearance—those men added nothing to my message" (Galatians 2:6). Like the person of Christ, Paul was not a man pleaser. He refused to allow pride to rule his life. Paul possessed a single heart focus of obedience to his Lord. He knew the other side of the coin; he lived it until his Damascus road conversion. There was no looking back for Paul. There was nothing good to return to.

On the contrary, we speak as men approved by God to be entrusted with the gospel. We are not trying to please men but God, who tests our hearts. You know we never used flattery, nor did we put on a mask to cover up greed— God is our witness. We were not looking for praise from men, not from you or anyone else. As apostles of Christ we could have been a burden to you...(1 Thessalonians 2:4-6).

We'll discuss pride in a little more depth when, in Chapter Seven, we look at the area of false humility.

Personal Growth Assignment
Spend two minutes thanking God for delivering you from a struggle that you no longer have because He is King over that area of your life. Ask for nothing—focus on thanksgiving.

Meditation Scripture for Obedience
Hebrews 5:7-10

[1]   Mark 6:6
[2]   Matthew 19:3
[3]   Luke 16:14
[4]   Matthew 26:14-16
[5]   Matthew 26:65-67; 27:27-31
[6]   John 17:6
[7]   John 17:8
[8]   John 17:10
[9]   John 17:12
[10] John 17:14
[11] John 17:18
[12] John 17:22
[13] John 17:26
[14] Larry Kreider, *The Cry for Spiritual Fathers and Mothers*, (Ephrata, PA: House to House Publications, 2000), p.26.

Icebreaker

Have each person in the group state one way he or she fulfills the role as a "master" (one in authority) and one way he or she is a "slave" (one in full submission) in his/her life.

Discussion Questions

1. Talk about one struggle you used to have that has been overcome now that you care more about what God thinks than what other people think.

2. Read John 8:14. Jesus obeyed the Father because His identity was found in His Father. Where do you look for your identity?

3. Are you more comfortable with someone who has not accepted Christ as their Savior, but obeys the Bible through "good, clean living," or would you rather be with someone who loves God first, but struggles in a few areas of obedience?

4. Discuss how pride in your own life is often connected to disobedience.

5. How does this disobedience keep you from accepting God's loving correction in your life?

Concluding Activity

Remain in the large group. Take two or three meditative minutes for each individual to come up with ways they have been more like a Pharisee than like Jesus. After time's up, allow for sharing and repentance. Each person who is willing to share should have a corresponding time of corporate prayer blessing. The cell leader, after this time of blessing, can speak scripture over the person. (1 John 1:9, 1 John 1:7, 1 John 3:7, 1 John 4:10 are all good places to start.)

Obedience Protects Me

It's hard to grasp what "wolves in our midst" are in this world, but I learned at 16 that I didn't have to fear them. I was newly liberated with my driver's license, a job, and the freedom of using my grandparents' 15 year-old car.

I was on my short drive home from work, thinking about what I needed to do that evening, when I stopped at a stop sign on a side street, waiting to make a turn. The next moment, I felt a nudge, thump and bump that moved me forward in my seat belt. Instinctively, I looked in my rear view mirror. Right behind me was a car with two men, the driver hitting his head with his hand as if he couldn't believe he had been so careless.

I knew what the driver's manual said to do in case of an accident. I could almost see the paragraph in my mind about exchanging driver's licenses and insurance information. But something told me to "just go." So I did. I watched in my rear view mirror at their astonished faces, and was sure my mother would be mad at me for not following the rules.

Two days later, we read a warning in the paper about several reports of two men targeting women riding alone in cars and causing accidents and much worse. I told my mother right then of God's goodness to me, and have walked in confidence since.

6

The Good News About Holiness

Do you know that the wicked will not inherit the kingdom of God? Do not be deceived: Neither the sexually immoral nor idolaters nor adulterers nor male prostitutes nor homosexual offenders nor thieves nor the greedy nor drunkards nor slanderers nor swindlers will inherit the kingdom of God. And that is what some of you were. But you were washed, you were sanctified, you were justified in the name of the Lord Jesus Christ and by the Spirit of God (1 Corinthians 6:9-11).

This scripture is a vivid picture of what we were. But, we were washed, sanctified, and justified in the name of Jesus and by the Spirit. How did this occur? A look at several other scriptures will reveal the answer to us:

For he chose us in him before the creation of the world to be holy and blameless in his sight (Ephesians 1:4).

How much more, then, will the blood of Christ, who through the eternal Spirit offered himself unblemished to God, cleanse our consciences from acts that lead to death, so that we may serve the living God! (Hebrews 9:14)

Only Christ can change a heart

The sacrifices of animals for sin was a temporary offering which did not change the heart toward obedience or holiness. Christ became the final sacrifice.

The law is only a shadow of the good things that are coming, not the realities themselves. For this reason it [the Law] can never, by the same sacrifices repeated endlessly year after year, make perfect those who draw near to worship. If it could, would they not have stopped being offered? The worshipers would have been cleansed once for all, and would no longer have felt guilty for their sins. But those sacrifices were an annual reminder of sins, because it is impossible for the blood of bulls and goats to take away sins.

Therefore, when Christ came into the world, he quoted Psalms 40:6-8 to prove that His voluntary and obedient sacrifice is better than the involuntary animal sacrifices in the Old Testament: "Sacrifice and offering you did not desire, but a body you prepared for me; with burnt offerings and sin offerings you were not pleased. Then I said, 'Here I am—it is written about me in the scroll—I have come to do your will, O God'" (Hebrews 10:5-7). God set aside the first to establish the second.

We have been made holy "once for all"

One other scripture from this chapter is, I believe, the capstone for us when it comes to how we become holy. This holiness begins with our complete belief and trust in the One who became the "second" in order to re-establish the beneficial truth of the first. This last scripture reveals that it would take a "final sacrifice." This type of sacrifice would literally rip the heart right out of a parent. It would cause a grief that could not be described with mere words. Let's read Hebrews 10:10 together: "And by that will, *we have been made holy* through the sacrifice of the body of Jesus Christ *once for all.*"

Grace says that He loves us so much there is nothing we can do on our own but to receive His grace and His holiness. Could we stop right now and pray to receive this free gift? Can you take a step of faith and pray this prayer?

"Dear Heavenly Father, I recognize that it is by Your grace that I am what I am and who I am today. It is by Your grace that I have received your Son into my heart and life. It is by Your grace that I am forgiven of my sin and placed in right-standing with You. Further, it is by Your grace that I have been made holy as it states in Your word in Colossians 1:22,23, "But now [You] have reconciled [me] by Christ's physical body through death to present [me] holy in [Your] sight, without blemish and free from accusation."

Since the cross of Calvary, God has desired a dwelling place within the heart of man. This place is made holy by the "holy One,"

Jesus Christ. Our desire must be to pursue holiness. You may have good intentions for holiness but good intentions are not enough. John Bevere in his book, *A Heart Ablaze*, puts it this way, "Desires and intentions are two different things, although many believe they are one and the same. You can have very good or godly intentions, but they may not be your true desires."[1] Is holiness your true desire?

Personal Growth Assignment

Read aloud Colossians 1:21, 22, substituting "I" for "you." Read it again, meditating on how this truth can set you free. Read it one last time, as a prayer for this season in your life.

Meditation Scripture for Obedience

1 Peter 1:14

[1] John Bevere, *A Heart Ablaze*, Thomas Nelson Publishers, Nashville, Tennessee, 1999.

Icebreaker

Have the people tell one thing they have "set to the side" or removed from normal use in order to be obedient to God.

Discussion Questions

1. Discuss, as a group, how the truth found in the first half of this book has caused a change in your behavior.

2. Discuss how you are closer to understanding God's love since beginning this study.

3. Read Hebrews 10:10. Discuss any personal revelation concerning personal holiness that you may have received since reading the scriptures about holiness.

4. What does 1 Corinthians 6:9-11 say happened when we gave our lives to Jesus? How did this happen? (Read Ephesians 1:4 and Hebrews 9:14).

5. Discuss the difference between desire and intention. Can you give an example of the difference from your life?

Concluding Activity

Remain in the large group. Go around the group in prayer. Have the person to the right of the cell leader pray for the person to his/her left.

Disobedience Soils Me

Holiness. Can we ever "feel" holy or righteous? I was driving to town one day alone on a back country road. There in the middle of the yellow lines was a magazine flapping in the wind. I've seen them before, mostly when I was a young boy riding my bike. I pull my car to the side of the road and get out to walk back to the glossy pages. I could turn around and leave. Why don't I? I'm telling myself it could be a news magazine or a hunting periodical. However, that would be a slim chance: people do not normally discard those magazines this way, and I know it.

I pick it up and discover that it is what I thought it was. My flesh longs to gaze at the color photos, my spirit is crying out, "No!" I could throw it to the side of the road and not look, but that would be littering. I know what I'll do: I'll dispose of it properly so no one else finds it and is tempted, especially a child.

I get into my vehicle. It won't hurt to take a peek—just to see what has changed since I was a kid. I stay there in my car, captivated by the explicitness, the color, the beauty, the flesh. My eyes are connecting to ink dots on a page. My mind is wandering. My flesh is tingling. My spirit is feeling soiled, dark, lost, disappointed, questioning who is this person holding this trash between his fingers? I disobeyed my Lord. I failed Him.

I open the passenger side window and throw it from my life, making a vow to never look at such demonically inspired material again.

I can show you where I stopped the car that dreadful day. I can still see some of those images in my mind even as I write this. How disgusted I felt with myself then—how free I feel today to have kept that vow. Obedience, it's worth it.

Humility—The Way To Holiness

A good friend of mine once shared with me what he felt was the reason for experiencing an emotional breakdown in his life. He came into my office one day and announced, "I know why."

"You know why what?" I questioned.

"I know why I went through all that I went through," he replied. After months of trying to break free of his dark, emotional struggle, the answer finally came. What was the answer? His response to me came in the form of one word—pride. My friend went on to share that pride was so much a part of his life, his way of thinking, that God allowed him to come to a place of humility in order to bring him to a place of obedience.

Pride is false humility

As we have previously discussed in chapter five, pride has a strong connection to disobedience. Proverbs tells us, "I (God) hate pride and arrogance" (Proverbs 8:13). Perhaps one reason God hates pride is that pride is false humility. False humility keeps us from walking in true humility which, in turn, keeps us from reaching our goal of true holiness.

Have you ever wondered why certain religions or cults stress a form of dress, often very plain in appearance? While it may have begun as an outward form of humility and piety, it can quickly turn the corner and become false humility. Colossians 2:18-23 does a great job defining legalism as false humility:

> Do not let anyone who delights in false humility and the worship of angels disqualify you for the prize. Such a person goes into great detail about what he has seen, and his unspiritual mind puffs him up with idle notions. He has lost connection with the Head, from whom the whole body, supported and held together by its ligaments and sinews,

grows as God causes it to grow. Since you died with Christ to the basic principles of this world, why, as though you still belonged to it, do you submit to its rules: "Do not handle! Do not taste! Do not touch!" These are all destined to perish with use, because they are based on human commands and teachings. Such regulations indeed have an appearance of wisdom, with their self-imposed worship, their false humility and their harsh treatment of the body, but they lack any value in restraining sensual indulgence.

Pride in disguise

A humble heart shows a submissive respect to God's desires, knowing that obeying His requests will produce satisfying fruit for both the giver and the recipient. A heart that is not humble desires attention or positive reaction either overt or subtle. This heart believes it knows what it needs to be satisfied and pursues it via earthly means. This false humility is pride in disguise.

False humility can take many different forms. The statements below are ones that have been thought, said or often heard. As you read over the list, ask God to search your heart and reveal to you any statements that perhaps you have used. Remember, it is not the statement itself that makes one falsely humble, it is the heart attitude:

- "The car I drive didn't make me go into debt."
- "I'd love to have a new sofa, but we gave money to the missionaries this month."
- "I won't capitalize my name anymore because Jesus is so much higher than me."
- "I have fasted one day a week for the last seven years. How much do you fast?"
- "I bought these clothes at the Salvation Army. Could you imagine paying three times this much buying it at a retail store?"
- "I won't eat meat, because the food fed to animals in America could feed thousands across the world."
- "I've had this _____ (fill in the blank) for 15 years now. It's still perfectly good."
- "I always reuse the back sides of paper. It's wasting them not to."

- "Saying you're humble means you're proud of being humble, and therefore, you're not humble. I don't make any bones about the fact that I'm not humble."
- "My wife doesn't work because it would be wrong for my children not to have their mother during the day."
- "I've never bought a new piece of furniture. All of my furnishings were given to me or come from secondhand stores or auctions."
- "I could pay full price for that, but instead I'll buy this lesser item and just make do."
- "I carry my Bible everywhere I go. Do you?"
- "Last year I witnessed to 30 people and five of them got saved. How many did you witness to?"
- "I will only homeschool my children, because I don't want to expose them to wrong influences in the public schools."
- "I wouldn't want to homeschool my children because who would be light in the darkness of public schools?"
- "No, please don't compliment my singing/speaking/good deed. It's just God working through me to bless you."
- "I won't let any of my daughters wear makeup or stylish fads, because the Bible says that beauty is not supposed to be on the outside."
- "I don't wear any dresses that have a V-neckline, so I don't cause my brothers to fall into sin."
- "As a Christian woman, I could never bring attention to myself. That runs counter to what Paul writes in the Bible about women."
- "My family has devotions every night together. How many nights does your family meet?"
- "I'm so glad that at least my children behave in church."
- "Do you still believe that? I used to, but God showed me something different."

Humility brings us to holiness and obedience

False humility yearns for the praise of men rather than walking in the approval of God. Romans 12:3 reveals to us, "For by the grace given me I say to every one of you: Do not think of yourself more highly than you ought, but rather think of yourself with sober judgement, in accordance with the measure of faith God has given you."

Secondly, the scriptures state, "A man's pride brings him low" (Proverbs 29:23a). Nebuchadnezzar, spoken of in the book of Daniel, is an interesting example of how low one can actually go. Nebuchadnezzar had a dream about a very large tree. He called upon Daniel to interpret his dream. Daniel reveals to Nebuchadnezzar that he was the tree, a tree so large that it was "visible to the whole earth" (Daniel 4:20). This tree represented Nebuchadnezzar's own pride and arrogance.

Daniel appeals to this leader in verse 27, "Renounce your sins, do what is right...renounce your wickedness...be kind to the oppressed...." Instead, King Nebuchadnezzar walks on the roof of his royal palace in Babylon saying to himself, "Is not this the great Babylon I have built...by my mighty power...for the glory of my majesty...?" (verse 30).

Little did Nebuchadnezzar realize what was about to happen to him. While those powerful words were still on his lips, a metamorphosis takes place, and he becomes like the beasts of the field—eating grass, hair growing all over his body and his nails becoming like claws of birds (verse 33). What is Daniel's explanation for this occurrence? Look at Daniel 5:20, "But when his [Nebuchadnezzar's] heart became arrogant and hardened with pride, he was disposed from his royal throne and stripped of his glory."

King Herod in Acts chapter twelve made a decision to begin persecuting the early church leaders. Jailing Peter and killing James with the sword pleased the Jews. Beyond the King's control, an angel releases Peter from prison. Herod was so upset that he had the guards executed. Peter's "escape" foiled his plan to place Peter on trial publicly. Herod then leaves for Caesarea and on an appointed day, wearing his royal robe, sitting on his throne, he delivers what must have been a captivating address. The audience responds, "This is the voice of a god, not a man" (verse 22). What follows is sobering. Verse 23 states, "Immediately, because Herod did not give praise to God, an angel of the Lord struck him down and he was eaten by worms and died."

It seemed that in both of these examples God was not impressed. Their hearts were full of pride and while they desired the praise of man for their accomplishments both King Nebuchadnezzar and King Herod breathed their last breath shouting their own personal accolades.

In Pursuit of Obedience

Humility can bring us to a place of holiness and obedience. Let's make that choice for ourselves so that God does not need to step in like a medical doctor and prescribe a large dose of humility. Jesus said it this way: "For whoever exalts himself will be humbled, and whoever humbles himself will be exalted" (Matthew 23:12).

Personal Growth Assignment

Review again the list of statements people use when they are being falsely humble. Place a check beside all those you have said to yourself in the last three months. Tell God and ask Him to meet the need that is causing you to want this self-encouragement. Listen quietly and ask Him to encourage you instead.

Meditation Scripture for Obedience

Hebrews 4:6; 11:8

Icebreaker

**SMALL GROUP
INTERACTION**

Have each person look to the person on his/her left and say, "This chapter is for you." Now have each person turn to the person on his/her right and say, "This chapter is for you."

Discussion Questions

1. Who in your group has conquered the pride issue in his/her life? Excuse that person to go get ice cream for the rest of the group, and continue on to question number two!

2. Which of the statements in the "Pride in disguise" section of this chapter are you most accustomed to hearing? Which ones are you most likely to say?

3. Which statements do you feel are not statements of false humility? Why? Can you write more statements reflecting false humility?

4. Read Romans 12:3 and Proverbs 29:23. How should we think of ourselves and what can result when pride sets in? How was the proud ruler Nebuchadnezzar brought low? (Daniel 4:19-33).

Concluding Activity

Break into groups of two: close friends, married couples, engaged couples. (The individual should be comfortable and familiar with his/her partner.) Each person in the subgroup should share an area of pride illuminated by this chapter. After this private confession, pray. The person who shared can ask forgiveness of God for his/her sin and ask that God show him/her who he/she has hurt by this pride, and for the courage to ask for forgiveness. His/her partner should pray for continued growth in this area. Read Psalm 139:23,24 aloud as a prayer for that person. Repeat for second person.

In Pursuit of Obedience

Cheating College Freshman

My feet felt like concrete as I walked along the slightly inclined path towards Dr. Barnett's office during his regular office hours. "Maybe he won't be in. Maybe he is out of town on a research project. Maybe there would be a long line of other students in front of me," I thought. "Maybe God is just testing me like he did Abraham by asking him to sacrifice his son. Abraham didn't really have to do it, right? God couldn't really want me to confess to my college professor that I had cheated on exams last year? My whole college career was at stake. What if Dr. Barnett had me thrown out of college? How would I explain that to my parents? How would I explain it to anyone for that matter?

I didn't want to, but I was going to see my Chemistry professor from my first year of college. I had all kinds of rationalizations for not doing what I knew in my heart God was telling me to do. Freshman Chemistry was a weed-out course for engineering students in our state college system. It was designed to be difficult to discourage freshman engineering students who either could not academically withstand the rigorous engineering curriculum or didn't have the discipline to make it through.

As a young college student trying to survive freshman chemistry, I would complete as many questions on the exam as I could do, but then my eyes would wander to try to find a neighboring student who had an answer for one of the questions I couldn't complete. The other students could have been guessing too, for all I knew. But the truth remained...I was getting answers from their test papers. It was cheating. I had cheated. Cheating was not allowed at the university where I attended or at any university. That was the point the Holy Spirit was making as I questioned why He was asking me to go back and confess to the professor. It could literally be the end of my college career, at least at that college.

Between my freshman and sophomore years of college, I had made Jesus the Lord of my life. In my mind, that meant that I was no longer the boss of my own life. It meant giving up college if that was what He wanted me to do. So, if I was thrown out of college for cheating I had no doubt that He had other plans for me. I had already thought through the whole thing and decided to go and confess to my chemistry teacher. That was a hard enough decision for me to make while praying in my bedroom at home, but the walk to

continued

his office was even worse.

One heavy foot followed the other as I made my way to the science building. As I turned the corner and my eyes fell on his open door, I almost bolted. But he saw me as soon as I turned the corner and welcomed me in. There was no turning back now.

The only thing I could do was get right to the point. I was so nervous and by this time sweaty, I don't even remember my exact words as I described to him what I had done the previous year. I did say that my life was changing because of a relationship with God and I had to make this right, no matter what happened. I finished talking and waited for his response.

To my surprise, he did not throw me out of the school. His words were, "I think your coming here is punishment enough. I won't take any further action." He said a bunch of other things too, but I don't remember what they were, because the burden of shame and guilt and possible expulsion from college were lifted. The next thing I knew I was shaking his hand on the way out the door. As I walked out the door and away from the science building my feet seemed light now. I felt like walking on air. I was not going to be dismissed from college, but more importantly I had obeyed God. What a good feeling!

Right Reasons
To Obey

I can firmly say that it can be challenging for me to obey Jesus at times. God, who created man and watched his downfall into selfishness in the Garden, knows this about His human creation. He understands perfectly how we tick and our motivations for following Him. In His abundant mercy, He created a beautiful cycle that allows us to grow to love Him in a pure, unselfish way. A good way to start this cycle is to understand where obedience takes us.

Obeying because we love God

I am trying to clarify that obedience is something to be done because of the loving relationship you have with God, not for what you can gain from God. Obedience is not something you do for obedience's sake only. God knew it would be hard for us, so He makes certain we know throughout scripture and everyday life that good things come from obedience.

The main reasons I don't (or am tempted not to) obey God are because I'm comfortable where I am, I'm afraid, I'm confused or I'm doubtful. What I'm failing to see in those times is the truth that God is a god of *abundance*. When He gives, He gives liberally. It is far beyond what we ask or imagine. He does this because His goal is to have us healthy spiritually, emotionally and physically for the sake of our relationship with Him and His purposes in the kingdom.

As always, scripture presents many stories of people who were just like us so we can learn from them and they can help us make good choices. These were persons who believed God and if we truly believe, we will obey. John Bevere wrote a brief commentary on 1 Peter 2:6-8a.

A peculiar statement appears in these verses. Peter says, "To you who believe...but to those who are disobedient."

He contrasts the words believe and disobey. We cannot do that today. Currently, the word believe has nothing to do with obedience or disobedience. That is why many within the church do not emphasize obedience. However, in the days of the New Testament writers they were closely connected. To believe meant not only to acknowledge His existence but also to obey. In other words, if you believed, you obeyed, and the evidence of not believing was a disobedient life-style.[1]

Let's look at some of these people and see where their obedience took them.

Obeying God when it risks our comfort

Do you remember the story of Elisha in 2 Kings 4, when God provides for Elisha through a wealthy woman who has no son? Elisha first prophesies that she will get pregnant with a son (she does), and then later raises him to life after the boy dies. Elisha's contact with that woman doesn't stop there. In 2 Kings 8:1-3, he meets her again and tells her to leave her home and land because a famine is coming that will put her and her family in danger. She does just that: she leaves her comfortable home, food, and friends to live in a foreign land. After seven years, she returns. Her obedience paid off. She and her family didn't starve when everyone she knew back home did. But what is even more interesting in this passage is found in verses 4-6:

> The king was talking to Gehazi, the servant of the man of God, and had said, "Tell me about all the great things Elisha has done." Just as Gehazi was telling the king how Elisha had restored the dead to life, the woman whose son Elisha had brought back to life came to beg the king for her house and land. Gehazi said, "This is the woman, my lord the king, and this is her son whom Elisha restored to life." The king asked the woman about it, and she told him. Then he assigned an official to her case and said to him, "Give back everything that belonged to her, including all the income from her land from the day she left the country until now."

Not only did the woman have her basic needs provided for in a very challenging time for her land, but she received back the property she had deserted and any income from the land for the seven years she had been gone!

The next time we are faced with the decision to obey God, even when it risks our comfort, let's remember this Shunammite woman who, after she obeyed, had her basic needs met and then reaped double.

Obeying God when we're afraid

In 2 Chronicles 20, King Jehoshaphat is in trouble. The Moabites, Ammonites, and some Meunites are in a vast army coming to make war against Judah. His prayer in verses 6-12 is a humble petition to ask God to save him. Jehoshaphat was afraid, just like all the inhabitants of Judah.

God hears Jehoshaphat's prayer and speaks to the assembly through Jahaziel: "Do not be afraid or discouraged because of this vast army" (verse 15). He goes on to give instructions and again addresses their fear with encouragement in verse 17. Jehoshaphat then obeys the battle instructions and, with praise, goes out and watches his enemy be destroyed without having to fight the battle at all. Isn't that great?

But again, God's very nature of abundance is revealed. Not only are they delivered, but the army of Judah then gets all the spoils of the battle. Verse 25 says it took three days to collect all the plunder! God not only eased the fear of those in Judah, but after Jehoshaphat obeyed, He destroyed a vast enemy army and further allowed Judah to be much richer for it. Is that not incredible? But wait! There's more! In verse 29 we further see that every kingdom around Judah heard about what happened. Now it was their turn to be afraid, and "the Kingdom of Jehoshaphat was at peace" (verse 30). Jehoshaphat was a wise ruler, indeed, to turn to the Lord in his distress, but he was wiser still to obey Him, despite how desperate the situation looked.

We would do well to remember Jehoshaphat the next time we are afraid for our lives, our reputations, or our welfare. Obedience preserved him and also blessed him with riches and peace.

Obeying God when we're confused or doubtful

The story of Lazarus' resurrection in John 11 is incredible. Jesus hears about Lazarus' sickness, but waits and doesn't show up in Bethany until days after Lazarus has died. Martha and Mary both know that Jesus could have healed their sick brother. When the time comes and Jesus commands the people to remove the stone from the grave, Martha pipes up, "But Lord...by this time there is a bad odor, for he has been there four days" (verse 39).

Remember, Jews did not embalm, so people removed dead animals and people as quickly as possible to avoid contaminating themselves and their possessions with decaying matter, and possibly causing sickness. What Jesus was asking these people to do not only went against their religious practice, but, excuse me, the odor from the grave would be pungent! They knew what they were facing when they removed that stone, and it included possibly losing their lunch as well as defiling themselves. To become clean again after being defiled was a lengthy, time-consuming process that affected the whole family. It was not desirable to become defiled.

However, we see that in verse 41, they took away the stone. They obeyed. It made no sense whatsoever; it meant considerable inconvenience and jeopardy of their welfare. But Jesus commanded and they obeyed. And what was the result of their obedience? Verse 44 states that "the dead man came out." Mary and Martha, good, faithful Jewish women, received back the love of their brother and their means of provision. What can compare with the majesty of this miracle? And yet, again, there is still more! In addition to receiving their heart's desire, they had the joy of seeing more people come to faith because of this miracle (verse 45).

Obeying God with only a promise

Hebrews 11 is known as the "faith" chapter of the Bible. It contains stories of obedient believers. One of those, Abraham, was called to an inheritance. The Scripture states in verse eight that he obeyed and went even though he didn't know where he was going. By faith this man, even though he was "past age," had a son. The promise from his obedience would be: "From this one man, and he as good as dead, came descendants as numerous as the stars in the sky and as countless as the sand on the seashore" (verse 12).

In Pursuit of Obedience

Abraham obeyed and saw Isaac. It's hard to even imagine that an entire nation would be birthed from this obedience, but it was because our God is a god of abundance!

Personal Growth Assignment

God created a cantaloupe vine to yield 4-8 fruits at maturity. Each vine requires only one seed to grow. Purchase a cantaloupe, cut it open, and calculate how many fruits could be produced if every seed were planted. Carry a seed with you to remind you that if He can do it with a cantaloupe, how much more will He abundantly provide for you!

Meditation Scripture for Obedience

Deuteronomy 11:26-28

1   John Bevere, *A Heart Ablaze*, Thomas Nelson Publishers, Nashville, Tennessee, 1999, p.24

SMALL GROUP INTERACTION

Icebreaker

Go around the group and have each person name the one commandment of the Ten Commandments they wish everyone in the world would follow all the time.

Discussion Questions

1. When is it most difficult for you to obey God: when you think your physical or emotional comfort will be jeopardized, when you are afraid, or when you are confused or doubtful?

2. Talk about a time when you were feeling this way, but responded in obedience and saw the result to be one of abundance in return.

3. Talk about a time when you were feeling this way, responded in obedience, but didn't see an abundant response in return. Let each member of the group state a way they see abundance in this instance.

4. Discuss the following scenario: What happens when you act upon what you thought was obedience to God only to find out it was your own emotions speaking?

5. Of the right reasons to obey God, what are several that you now realize you must work on and maintain accountability to follow through with?

Concluding Activity

Get into a circle. Since the group members have already stated when it is most difficult for them to obey God, call all the people who stated it was their physical or emotional comfort to sit in the middle of the circle. Allow time for members on the outside ring to pray for this group corporately. Speak blessings of abundance and reminders of existing abundance over this group. Repeat for the "afraid" group and the "confused/doubtful" group.

Obedience Pays Off

A friend of mine in his early twenties was in a farm partnership with his father. As an only son, his father's desire was to help him become prosperous in business with the opportunity to make millions of dollars through the family farm. But he felt drawn by the Lord to focus much of his time helping people come into relationship with Christ. Starting with helping troubled teenagers, with his wife and a small team of others, they discipled new believers while he continued to serve with his father on the family farm partnership. But eventually, my friend had to make a decision. He did not have time for both. He obeyed the call of God, gave up the farm partnership in obedience to God and started a new church for new believers. Today, more than 20 years later, my friend serves in an international ministry along with his associates on five continents of the world. And that's not all. Someone recently gave him a farm! Our God is a God of abundance, desiring to bless His children who walk in obedience to Him!

More Reasons
To Obey

In the same way that you would not want to disappoint someone you love and care for very much, it would be your heart's desire, your soul's intent, and your spirit's willingness to be so committed to God you would never want to disappoint Him.

My children obey me because they love me. We are in relationship—a relationship of love. They know I'm committed to them and no matter what they do, I'll still love them.

One day, my wife and I and our son, Joshua, found ourselves sitting before a district magistrate, listening to her "throw the book at him" with a harsh tone of voice. You could just feel a spirit of shame spewing forth as Joshua cringed at her words with his head lowered and large crocodile tears dropping from his 15-year-old eyes.

My son had a minor brush with the law and his consequence was appropriate. Finally, when the judge was finished with him, I became her target. I didn't mind because it gave me an opportunity to say what I wanted to speak from my heart. "Your Honor," I began, "what my son did was wrong and he will pay the deserved consequences. But, I want to establish right here and now that I love my son. In fact, I love him more today than yesterday. Most of all, your Honor, I want him to know that God loves him very much and that this incident does not change God's love for him."

I knew the Lord enabled me to say these things. The judge was somewhat caught off-guard by my profession of unconditional love for my son: "Well, yes, of course. I do not expect to see you or your son here again," she concluded quickly.

Chuck Colson, in his book *How Now Shall We Live,* illustrates this love when he shares about an encounter that he had with the Minister of Justice in the nation of Bulgaria. The minister felt that fear would keep people from disobeying the law. Colson responded,

"No, sir! Fear does not stop people. If it did, no one would smoke (cigarettes)." Colson went on to say, "Only love changes human behavior. If I love another person, I want to please him or her; if I love God, I want to please Him and do what He wants. Only love can overcome our sinful self-centeredness."[1]

In the same way, you are lovingly and completely committed to your children or a loved one, strive to maintain a single heart commitment to loving your God through obedience.

> Jesus replied, "If anyone loves me, he will obey my teaching. My Father will love him, and we will come to him and make our home with him. He who does not love me will not obey my teaching. These words you hear are not my own; they belong to the Father who sent me" (John 14:23,24).

You love and are committed to God's Word

To obey God fully, you must trust His Word as your source of truth. You must believe that all of God's Word is true and that He stands behind this Book. There are many books of truth written today. Only one of those contains inspired truth.

It never ceases to amaze me that the people whom I counsel often comment about how I use God's Word in the counseling process. I find myself wondering, "What would I say, what would I counsel, what boundaries could I discuss, what rules for holy living could I invent without God's Word?"

God's Word cannot be looked at as an old, outdated volume of stories. It is more current than tomorrow's newspaper. It reveals the heart of God to His people. If you desire to walk in obedience, desire more of God's Word in your life. Consume it daily as you do any physical meal.

"Then you will know the truth and the truth will set you free" (John 8:32). Jesus prayed to His Father for us about this truth in John 17:17 saying, "Sanctify them by the truth; your word is truth."

You desire to walk in humility

"Pride goes before destruction..." (Proverbs 16:18). To walk in humility is to walk in obedience to God. Let's look at the leader Moses once again. I believe the reason for his great leadership is found in Numbers 12:3, "Now Moses was a very humble man,

In Pursuit of Obedience

more humble than anyone else on the face of the earth." Moses' leadership was not necessarily about his giftedness. In fact, we know that Moses struggled with his own ability to speak (Exodus 4:10).

The secret to Moses' success as a leader was his quick willingness to obey his heavenly Father. Even when all of the children of Israel raised complaints and questions with him, he faithfully obeyed God, walked in the miraculous, and saw the deliverance of his people from the Egyptians. Moses' walk of humility had tremendous world-changing benefits.

You want to expose false humility and legalism in your life

God is not a legalist. Jesus became a curse for us so that we no longer need to follow the curse of the law. Galatians 3:13 states, "Christ redeemed us from the curse of the law by becoming a curse for us, for it is written: 'Cursed is everyone who is hung on a tree.'"

It was the Pharisees that tried to hang onto the law along with their many legalistic ways. This was not obedience to Jesus. Perhaps you were initially scared off from Christianity because you observed some form of false humility or legalism. While each culture and age group seems to have a certain form of acceptable dress and haircut, God has never looked at the outward appearance of a man and made any kind of judgment. Paul wrote, "God does not judge by external appearance" (Galatians 2:6).

God looks at the heart of a man. "God, who knows the heart, showed that he accepted them by giving the Holy Spirit to them, just as he did to us."[2] If in your heart you desire to obey Him, ask Him to expose any false humility and legalistic ways in your life.

Maybe you're an older Christian and you have some legalistic tendencies. Those false forms of humility can actually cause you to trust in your outward form and religion rather than the living God. Ask Him to expose these things in your life.

You want to enjoy God's freedom and favor

The person who is truly set free to obey God is the one who knows they are set free. Galatians 5:1 states, "It is for freedom that Christ has set us free..."

God desires freedom for you for freedom's sake. What wonderful and powerful words these are! In other words, freedom without expectation—He wants you to experience freedom because He loves you.

Some time ago, God graciously gave me a picture of myself locked in permanent shackles—shackles so tight I could not move. When I asked Jesus to forgive me of my sin and received Him into my heart, those tight-fitting, binding chains fell off of me with a loud clatter to the ground. I felt so light, and so free! I finally could walk, run, and jump effortlessly! I was released to experience the freedom of serving Christ.

The rebellious take freedom as a license to do whatever pleases their senses. The righteous take freedom as a means of liberty to be involved in what pleases God. As we choose to use our freedom to please God, we'll find favor with God.

We know that Daniel refused to stray from God's pattern for his life and consequently reaped great benefits. Daniel chapter one says that Daniel resolved not to defile himself, instead gaining permission from the officials to eat as he wished rather than eating the rich royal food and wine that dulled the mind. Subsequently, God gave Daniel knowledge of all kinds of literature and learning and also the ability to understand visions and dreams. In Daniel's obedience to His God he found God's favor, as well as man's favor, in his life (Daniel 1:8-20).

Personal Growth Assignment

Read Daniel 1. Say verses eight and nine aloud, replacing your name with "Daniel." Reflect on your feeling when you read these verses. Spend two or three minutes asking God to help you do the right thing when you aren't "feeling" like it. Ask the Holy Spirit to remind you of Daniel 1:8,9 when faced with the choice to obey or disobey.

Meditation Scripture for Obedience
Jeremiah 7:23

---

[1] Charles Colson, *How Now Shall We Live?* Wheaton, Illinois: Tyndale House Publisher, Inc.,1999.

[2] Acts 15:8

In Pursuit of Obedience

Icebreaker

Go around the group and ask each person to share one way their understanding of obedience has changed since beginning this study.

Discussion Questions

1. Of the five reasons to obey God listed in this chapter, which do you struggle with the most? The least?

2. What are some reasons to obey God that are not listed here?

3. What is an area to which you know God is calling you toward obedience?

4. Read John 14:23,24. Why is the love God has for us and that we have for Him crucial to understanding obedience?

5. Take a few minutes to read Psalm 73. How is this Psalm connected to the subject of obedience?

Concluding Activity

Divide into groups of four. Without any discussion, ask the groups to pray only prayers of praise (telling God who He is and speaking His attributes) for five minutes, remaining in silent prayer if they finish beforehand. After five minutes, ask each group to pray only prayers of repentance (stating errors they would like to change in their lives) related to the issues stated in this book, remaining in silent prayer if they finish beforehand. Then request each group to ask forgiveness for the things they just stated, remaining in silent prayer if they finish beforehand. Close as the Holy Spirit leads.

Was That You Lord?

I tend to ask this question when things do not work out the way I anticipated. Did I misunderstand what God asked me to do? Was the timing off by a decade? Was this my idea, and I construed it to be the will of the Lord? The truth is that God is more concerned about conforming our life into the image of His Son Jesus than helping us win at every Christian event we enter.

I opened two businesses to facilitate our mission efforts in a region. With the business came the purchase of a large piece of equipment for resale in our target nation. The equipment was purchased with investment money from the Christian business community. During the following year, we struggled financially as we faced massive debts. We prayed and saw little encouragement. We took jobs with the equipment to demonstrate its ability and cover some of the expenses. The workload was enormous. At a Christian conference during our financial struggles, a speaker prophesied over me. He saw me digging with my bare hands through a brick wall. He continued by saying that when I made it through the wall, I would find another wall, yet much thicker than the first. He concluded, "Do not be discouraged because it is all an illusion." Does God call us to dig through walls to find more walls in place?

A letter came from one investor requesting the return of his financial investment. There was little hope to return the money. I faced writing one of the hardest letters of my life. In the letter I told the investor that the money would be repaid, and asked for his patience. A sick feeling swept through me as I placed the letter in the mail. The next day the machine sold and the repayment to this investor was possible within a week of my asking for his patience! Then, an unexpected word came to me.

I sensed the Lord asking me to purchase a second piece of equipment. With the difficulties of the first sale, and financial loss incurred, why would we speculate on a second machine? I checked the understanding I had by praying with both our mission pastor and mission director. They both sensed from the Lord it was good to move ahead. Other investors were sought for the second piece of equipment, spare parts, shipping, import customs, etc. Bit by bit, we worked our way through the hurdles of shipping and importing. The financial outlay was significantly more than on the first machine.

continued

We were not only stretched, but in a place that tested us in many areas of faith. Then the nation's economy fell sharply.

People were not purchasing equipment of any size, especially larger equipment. I attempted to take jobs with the second machine like I did with the first one. There were no jobs. Our beautiful machine was silent, unused and aging. The words of the prophecy came back to my mind; the wall was thicker indeed. The thought kept coming to me, "What were you thinking when you purchased this machine?" The hammering assault is in the validity to hear God when pain, sickness or failure result from our obedience. I questioned if it was God's voice that led me to purchase this machine. I also questioned if the other two gentlemen I looked up to heard from the Lord or simply had confidence in me.

One morning, at a very low point in my life, I told God, "The place in which I find myself is impossible. People cannot afford the equipment; they do not like the system or the limitations it has, and they do not like the name of my company. This is impossible!" As I rounded the entrance of my home and touched the steps, revelation came that brought answers in the storm. The Lord asked me if we have food on our breakfast table, which of course we did. He asked me if my children were in school and the tuition paid, if the heating oil in my tank was keeping us warm, if the rent and utilities were paid. Embarrassed, I knew everything was covered. Then he spoke, "This is not impossible, you are just uncomfortable."

Obeying God with the qualification of gratification or success is hedonism. We learn obedience when life is uncomfortable. And then the cross seems to remind us more clearly of the price paid for our lives.

The Obedience Cycle

We cannot "out-give" God. Obedience reaps more than we can ask or imagine. Our lives are transformed when this concept of great returns for our obedience is instilled into our hearts by the Holy Spirit. In fact, it becomes a self-feeding cycle:

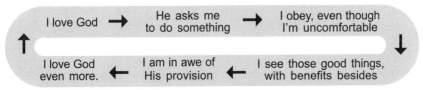

John 14:15 comes alive as we realize that obedience is a natural reaction from being cared for lovingly: "If you love me, you will obey what I command." God Himself is providing the motivation to obey and maintain our relationship with Him. Addictions lose their grip on our lives because we reject the object of our addictions, knowing we have not only healing, but wholeness awaiting us. Other people's opinions lose their sharpness, because we desire God's opinion of us, knowing it will be one of love. Fear loses its grip, and we trust more.

It comes down to what our inward motivation is. Many times throughout the Old Testament we see a leader of God attempting to convince an out of control children of God (Israel) to obedience. The problem is that we tend to gravitate toward what is found in our heart. Moses was a leader who fully desired to know his God and his leadership was a picture of that hunger. Israel on the other hand would get excited about obeying God, listening to God, or worshipping God when they discovered what He could do for them.

Often in obedience, we look for the thing that provides immediate gratification. But, how long can you or I pursue a life of faith, belief and obedience when we do not realize an immediate answer, especially an answer that may be different from the one we desire?

What if obedience does not bring the desired results?

There are times when obedience does not result in good upon good. You know stories of people who did the right thing and yet circumstances seemed to get worse for them. John the Baptist obeyed God in preparing the way for our Lord and was beheaded. Micaiah, in 1 Kings 22, prophesied the truth to King Ahab and ended up in prison for the rest of his life. In Genesis 39, Joseph obeyed God and found himself in prison for a long time.

Christians all over the world have lost everything (including their lives) because they obeyed God. Obedience in this light is truly the obedience "that comes from the heart," as is stated in Romans 6:17. We no longer have to dread obedience as a sacrifice of self, because we see what the bigger picture of obedience reaps.

Mahesh Chauda in his book, *The Hidden Power of the Believer's Touch*, makes an important point concerning obedience and what it requires: "Only through faith and obedience can any of us know the deep things of God... It requires patience and discipline, and a daily walking in the Spirit..."[1]

Obedience cannot be solely based upon reaching a desired end. God's desire in our obedience may be very different from what we have projected to be the result. I am reasonably sure that John the Baptist experienced a much different ending to his life on this earth than he could foresee or predict. While unexpected, he obeyed His heavenly Father to the end.

How do I get started?

Are you wanting to dig deeper into obedience? Here are some questions to ask yourself in order to help you prepare for your new pursuit:

- Am I pursuing an intimate relationship with God in my life? Is it the most intimate relationship that I have?
- Am I dealing with interferences to that intimacy (i.e., lack of proper understanding of intimacy, allowing circumstances or people to overwhelm me)?

- Do I, in my heart, desire to be obedient?
- Do I understand that obedience has multiple layers?
- Do I believe that God truly wants the best for me in my life and that He has my best interest in mind?
- Am I willing to admit I am wrong in some concepts of obedience? Am I asking God to show me His definition of obedience?
- Am I willing to stop making excuses, understanding that His boundaries are loving?
- Do I want to be "set apart," (the definition of holiness)?
- Am I willing to confess my errors in obeying God for the wrong reasons?
- Do I want to lay down my heavy burdens of legalism and obey for the right reasons?
- Am I willing to look at the false humility/pride in my life?
- Am I willing to look at the excuses I have been making for my disobedience?
- Am I ready and willing to not only listen to the word but to obey the word? (James 1:22)

Christ in us: our hope

My favorite scripture in the New Testament is found in Galatians, chapter two, verse twenty, "I have been crucified with Christ and I no longer live, but Christ lives in me. The life I live in the body, I live by faith in the Son of God, who loved me and gave himself for me." The revelation discovering that Christ, the Son of God, lives in me has got to be life changing. I know it was for me.

This verse became my favorite because through it I found the needed ingredient to move toward obedience. While the spirit is willing, the flesh is often weak. But, with Christ in me I can do all things—even obey! You see, once I was alienated from God in my mind and in my behavior. Christ became my reconciler and through His death I become "...holy in his sight, without blemish and free from accusation..." (see Colossians 1:21-23). Like Paul wrote in 2 Corinthians 12 when he discovered he could not rid himself of a thorn in his flesh, he became dependent upon God. To get started on the road to obedience is to know Christ's residence within you in such a way that it causes you to confess, "Lord, your power is made perfect in my weakness...for when I am weak, then I am strong" (1 Corinthians 12:9,10).

I can do everything through him who gives me strength (Philippians 4:13).

The Great Commission—obey what I command

The Great Commission mandates: "Go...make disciples...baptize them...and teaching them..." (Matthew 28:19, 20). Teaching them what? Read the rest of the verse to see Christ revealing something so important, so profound, and yet so simple: "...and teaching them to **obey** everything I have commanded you." The closing topic of the Gospel of Matthew, words of admonishment from our Lord Jesus, was about obedience.

By now I hope you realize why God wants you to obey Him. He loves you and desires to have a close, intimate relationship with you. The truth is that we will not always obey Him. When we sin, we fall short of God's glorious, grace-filled ideal. However, when we fail, our Savior, full of love, will forgive us (has forgiven us) and move us on from this point. Our part is to receive that forgiveness, get back up, run to Him, and choose to set our hearts once again toward obedience. He's waiting.

Obedience has its reward

Going back to my military experiences, I remember earning that coveted stripe so visible on my shoulders. It was a trademark that followed rigorous and what seemed like endless days of marching, running, military classes, and spit-shining shoes. Looking around, it was noticeable that not all fifty members of our squadron were present to enjoy the moment.

There was Parker who was sent to the "motivational flight" (the nice word for rebellious airmen). James and others were discharged due to failing the ongoing drug tests. And there were Williams and Bernouski who just broke down, lost it emotionally and physically fell apart. These guys did not make it. Some of them struggled with orders that seemed to make no logical sense. But, it was not for us to question—it was for us to obey. Those who endured were rewarded. Those who did not endure for one reason or another were soon missing from our ranks. As far as the military was concerned, those persons no longer existed. Many were discharged—not an honorable or desired finish.

I could not help but think of this time in my life in closing this book. There was something about that final parade for the graduation service. At that point, it did not concern us whether or not the orders barked out by our drill instructors made sense or not. Those moments were behind us. It was a time to be proud in a healthy sense of accomplishment, to be jubilant, to enjoy the moment and to look ahead to even greater rewards. It was the end of the "basic" and the beginning of normal military life.

Do you look forward to that final parade? Will you obey orders whether you understand or not? As a Christian, there is a future and a hope. While there may be tests to go through and obedience may take everything within us, it will be worth it. At that point, being told to enter into the joy of the kingdom will cause all of the trials and challenges of this world to fade. Our eyes will behold a new present and a new future. This reward for our obedience to the Gospel cannot be described through our finite perceptions.

My heart is for you and I to meet there. Until then, let's gather as many as we can to go with us, obeying and fulfilling the Great Commission.

Closing prayer for obedience

I hope this book has challenged you in your walk as a Christian. I think it is fitting to finish with Paul the apostle's words to Titus. It seems that loving God enough to obey Him was on his heart as well:

> Remind the people to be subject to rulers and authorities, to be obedient, to be ready to do whatever is good, to slander no one, to be peaceable and considerate, and to show true humility toward all men. At one time we too were foolish, disobedient, deceived and enslaved by all kinds of passions and pleasures. We lived in malice and envy, being hated and hating one another. But when the kindness and love of God our Savior appeared, he saved us, not because of righteous things we had done, but because of his mercy. He saved us through the washing of rebirth and renewal by the Holy Spirit, whom he poured out on us generously through Jesus Christ our Savior, so that, having been justified by his grace, we might become heirs having the hope of eternal life. This is a trustworthy saying. And I

want you to stress these things, so that those who have trusted in God may be careful to devote themselves to doing what is good. These things are excellent and profitable for everyone (Titus 3:1-8).

Take the time to sincerely pray this prayer and may God grant a spirit of obedience and holiness in your life until the day you enter the joys of heaven:

Father, at one time I lived in foolishness and disobedience to You and Your Word. My desires were filled with selfish ambition. But, because of Your love and Your grace, You have saved me through the washing of Your Word. You paid the penalty for my disobedience by being obedient all the way to the cross. I cannot repay You except to commit now to love and obey You. In Jesus' Name, Amen.

Personal Growth Assignment
Pull out the small taped sheets of paper you made after Chapter One. Reflect on whether your outlook on this boundary has changed. Obedience is a daily choice, and some days will be harder than others. Spend five minutes asking God to seal in you what you have learned and for a continuing revelation of both His deep and abiding love for you and how you can obey more each day.

Meditation Scripture for Obedience
Philippians 2:8

---

[1] Mahesh Chauda, *The Hidden Power of the Believer's Touch*, Destiny Image Publishers, Inc., Shippensburg, PA, 2001.

Icebreaker

SMALL GROUP INTERACTION

Go around the room and have each person state which they would rather do:

1. Invest in a savings plan that has a guaranteed return of 110%.
2. Plant a seed of a favorite food that had a guaranteed yield of 110%.
3. Buy a house that had a guaranteed appreciation of 110% when you chose to sell.

Discussion Questions

1. Do you agree with the cycle listed at the beginning of this chapter? If you do, state which part of the cycle is hardest for you to get through. If you don't, state what you think the cycle should say.

2. Read John 14:15 and discuss how obedience to God is demonstrating our love for God.

3. Share ways in which you are involved in fulfilling the Great Commission, and therefore, experiencing the fruit of obedience.

4. What are some good things in your life that obedience to God has reaped?

5. Can you give an example of a time that you chose to walk in obedience only to "suffer" for taking that step?

6. Talk about one thing from this book for which you desire your small group to hold you accountable for over the next six weeks.

Concluding Activity

Have a group prayer time about the items in Discussion Question #3. After completion, ask if there is anyone who would like to be held accountable for something related to obedience they are changing in their lives. Ask for volunteers for this accountability partnership.

In Pursuit of Obedience